The Tale of the Root Children

Etwas von den Wurzelkindern

Sibylle von Olfers

The Tale of the Root Children

Etwas von den Wurzelkindern

Translated into English
by
WALTER and NADINE SAUER

Edition Tintenfaß

D-69239 Neckarsteinach
Tel. / Fax: +49 - 62 29 - 23 22
www.verlag-tintenfass.de
info@verlag-tintenfass.de

Satz: OLD-Media, Heidelberg
Druck: Appel & Klinger, Schneckenlohe

ISBN 978-3-946190-14-1

Cover of the original edition

“Wake up, wake up, my children dear
For springtime is now almost here.”
The little root folk everywhere
Get up and stretch and comb their hair.

„Wacht auf, wacht auf, ihr Kinderlein,
es wird nun wohl bald Frühling sein!“
Da reckt und streckt die kleine Schar
und fährt sich durch das wirre Haar.

The little root girls are quite nimble
With scissors, needle, thread and thimble.
They make their dresses with much glee –
Such seamstresses you rarely see.

Schnell machen alle sich bereit
und nähn sich selbst ihr Frühlingskleid.
Mit Nadel, Schere, Fingerhut
geht ihre Arbeit schon ganz gut.

Then quickly all the children go
To Mother Earth and want to show
Their pretty dresses, stand in line
To hear her say: “Oh my, how fine.”

Nun kommt ein jedes Wurzelkind
und bringt sein Kleidchen ganz geschwind
hinein zur guten Mutter Erde,
damit’s von ihr gemustert werde.

And all the while you maybe ask:
What is the little root boys' task?
With paint and brush they go ahead,
Paint bugs and beetles black and red.

Die Wurzeljungen unterdessen
haben auch nicht ihr Amt vergessen:
Mit Pinsel, Bürste, Farbentopf
gehn sie den Käfern an den Schopf.

Rot
Schwarz

When springtime
finally does show
The little folk come
from below,
The beetles, grasses,
flowers bright
Are marching out,
a lovely sight.

The lilies of the valley there
Bloom in the woods, all white and fair.
A little snail is scared – and see:
The violet hides behind a tree.

Im Walde unterm dichten Grün
sieht man alsbald Maiglöckchen blühn.
Ein lust'ger Schelm die Schneck' erschreckt,
das Veilchen sich am Baum versteckt.

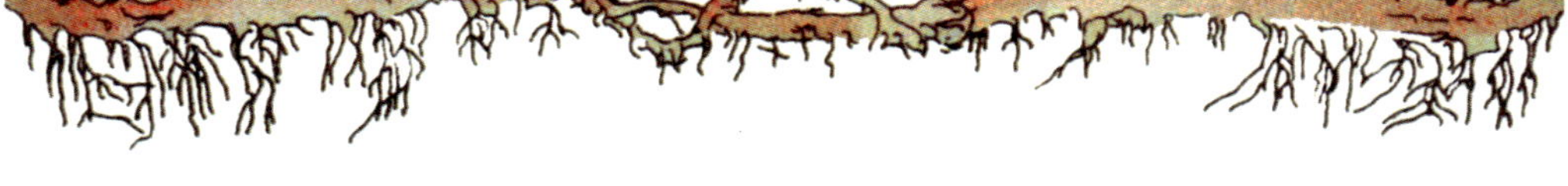

Und als der Frühling kommt ins Land,
da ziehn gleich einem bunten Band,
die Käfer, Blumen, Gräser klein
frohlockend in die Welt hinein.

Forget-me-nots play by a creek
At blind man’s bluff and hide and seek.
The water lily can be seen,
Her throne a leaf, just like a queen.

Es spielen hier den ganzen Tag
Vergissmeinnicht am klaren Bach;
wie eine kleine Königin
lässt ’s Mummelkind umher sich ziehn.

Down in the meadow hand in hand
The flowers dance, a happy band,
And with the beetles leap and bound.
It should be summer all year round.

Auf grüner Wies' am Feldesrand
die Blümlein tanzen Hand in Hand,
Gräslein und Käfer freun sich sehr,
ach, wenn's doch immer Sommer wär'!

When autumn comes with wind and rain
They rush to Mother Earth again.
"To bed, root children, and sleep tight
Till next year when the time is right."

Da kommt der Herbst mit Sturm und Wind,
treibt sie zur Mutter heim geschwind.
„Geh' nun zu Bett, du kleine Schar
und schlaf dich aus bis nächstes Jahr."

Sibylle von Olfers (1881 – 1916)
Photograph: Königsberg 1905

Afterword

Sibylle von Olfers' children's book *Etwas von den Wurzelkindern* is one of the best known German picture books, ranking with Heinrich Hoffmann's *Der Struwwelpeter*, Wilhelm Busch's *Max und Moritz* or *Die Häschenschule* by Fritz Koch-Gotha and Albert Sixtus. Its lasting popularity as a children's classic in Germany can easily be compared with that of *Mother Goose's Nursery Rhymes*, *Alice in Wonderland* or *Peter Rabbit* in English speaking countries.

Sibylle von Olfers was born on May 8, 1881 in Metgethen Castle near Königsberg, East Prussia (today Kaliningrad Oblast, Russia). She grew up and was educated on the family's estate and in Königsberg. At the age of 17, she moved to Berlin to be with her aunt, who had recognized Sibylle's artistic talent from her early childhood. There she continued her training as an artist. Having been a religious person all her life, she entered the convent of the "Sisters of Saint Elizabeth" in Königsberg at the age of 25, becoming Sister Maria Aloysia. In 1908, her order sent her to Lübeck to teach at the local Catholic elementary school.

Her first children's book, *Was Marilenchen erlebte*, appeared in 1905. Until her untimely death at only 34, she wrote and illustrated eight more children's books, among which *Etwas von den Wurzelkindern* (1906) was to become a classic of German children's literature. She died on January 29, 1916 of a pulmonary disease.

Although *Etwas von den Wurzelkindern* has been translated into Chinese, Czech, Dutch, Japanese, Russian, Slovenian and Spanish, it has never been adequately rendered into English verse. We are pleased to publish this translation along with the German original on the 100th anniversary of the author-illustrator's death and in the 110th year of its first publication.

The pictures have been reproduced from an early edition of the work (24th edition, c1930), which still retains the artist's original vibrant full page art nouveau illustrations.

Walter Sauer

29 January, 2016

Nachwort

Wie Heinrich Hoffmanns *Struwwelpeter*, Wilhelm Buschs *Max und Moritz* und *Die Häschenschule* von Fritz Koch-Gotha und Albert Sixtus gehört Sibylle von Olfers' *Etwas von den Wurzelkindern* zu den von der Mitte des 19. bis zum Beginn des 20. Jahrhunderts entstandenen klassischen deutschen Kinderbüchern. Sie haben alle Irrungen und Wirrungen der Pädagogik, der Kinderbuchkritik und des sich wandelnden Geschmacks unbeschadet überlebt und erfreuen immer noch neue Generationen von Kindern – und auch ältere Jahrgänge, die sich in nostalgischer Rückschau an die beliebte Lektüre ihrer Kindheit erinnern.

Sibylle von Olfers wurde am 8. Mai 1881 auf Schloss Metgethen bei Königsberg in Ostpreußen geboren. Sie wuchs auf dem Rittergut der Familie und in Königsberg auf. Mit 17 Jahren zog sie nach Berlin zu ihrer Tante, die schon in Sibylles Kindheit ihre zeichnerische Begabung erkannt und sie gefördert hatte. Dort setzte sie ihre künstlerische Ausbildung fort. Bereits seit ihrer Kindheit ein frommes Mädchen, trat sie mit 24 Jahren als Schwester Maria Aloysia in den Orden der „Schwestern von der Heiligen Elisabeth" in Königsberg ein. Im Jahre 1905 schickte sie der Orden als Schulschwester nach Lübeck, wo sie neben ihren pädagogischen Aufgaben an der Lübecker katholischen Volksschule auch vielfältig künstlerisch tätig war. Im selben Jahr wurde ihr erstes Kinderbuch, *Was Marilenchen erlebte*, veröffentlicht. Ihm folgten bis zu ihrem Tode weitere acht von ihr verfasste und illustrierte Kinderbilderbücher, darunter *Etwas von den Wurzelkindern* (1906), das zu einem Klassiker der deutschen Kinderliteratur werden sollte. Erst 34 Jahre alt, starb sie am 29. Januar 1916 in Lübeck an einem Lungenleiden.

Wir freuen uns, das reizende Kinderbuch im 100. Todesjahr seiner Verfasserin, der nur ein kurzes Leben beschieden war, in verschiedenen Sprachversionen vorlegen zu können. Als Grundlage unserer Neuausgabe diente ein gut erhaltenes frühes Exemplar des Buches (24. Auflage, ca. 1930; Kleine Ausgabe) aus unserer Kinderbuchsammlung, das im Gegensatz zu späteren Auflagen noch die vollständigen, originalen Jugendstilillustrationen aufweist.

Im Gegensatz zu Heinrich Hoffmanns *Struwwelpeter,* Wilhelm Buschs *Max und Moritz* und der *Häschenschule* von Fritz Koch-Gotha und Albert Sixtus ist Sibylle von Olfers' *Etwas von den Wurzelkindern* noch nie auf eine Art, die dem deutschen Original gerecht wird, in englische Verse übertragen worden. Hier erscheinen die »Wurzelkinder« nun 110 Jahre nach ihrem ersten Erscheinen in einer zweisprachigen englisch-deutschen Fassung.

Walter Sauer
29. Januar 2016

Dank des Verlags

Dank gebührt Herrn Tobias Rößler, der uns auf die 100. Wiederkehr des Todes von Sibylle von Olfers hinwies und uns mit einem schönen lateinischen Chronogramm erfreute. Wir dürfen es hier abdrucken.

The Publisher

wishes to thank Tobias Rößler, who pointed out to us the 100th anniversary of Sibylle von Olfers' death and kindly sent us the following Latin chronogram.

fabeLLa pICta
DE pVerVLIs et pVeLLVLIs
terrestrIbVs

IV kaL. febrVarIas
sIbyLLa DE oLfers
LVbeCae eX VIta CessIt

MCMXVI

Also available from Edition Tintenfaß:

ISBN 978-3-943052-27-5

ISBN 978-3-937467-94-8

ISBN 978-3-937467-21-4

ISBN 978-3-943052-35-0

ISBN 978-3-943052-08-4

ISBN 978-3-943052-75-6

ISBN 978-3-946190-10-3

ISBN 978-3-937467-54-2